The Jesus book

40 Bible stories retold by LaVonne Neff
and illustrated by Toni Goffe

Loyola Press

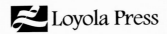

3441 North Ashland Avenue
Chicago, Illinois 60657

1999 first United States edition

Published in Great Britain by Hunt & Thorpe
Stories and illustrations previously published in
The Life of Christ for Children series

0-8294-1373-1

Contents

An Angel Visits Mary

Luke 1:26-38

There once was a girl named Mary who lived in a village called Nazareth. She was engaged to be married to a carpenter, Joseph. Mary was a good, sensible girl, and she never expected a visit from an angel.

But suddenly one day, without warning, the mighty angel Gabriel stood before her. "Greetings! The Lord is with you," Gabriel said.

Mary stepped back in fear. "Don't be afraid," said the angel. "You have found favor with God. You will have a son, and you will name him Jesus. He will be King forever."

"How can this be?" Mary asked. "I am a virgin."

Gabriel answered, "The Holy Spirit will make this happen. That is why your child will be called the Son of God."

Mary knew that God had sent the angel to her.

"I am the Lord's servant," she said. "Let it be to me as you have said."

Mary Visits Elizabeth

Luke 1:39-56

The angel Gabriel brought Mary good news about her cousin Elizabeth. Elizabeth had no children, and now she was old. "Soon Elizabeth will have a son," Gabriel said. "With God, nothing is impossible."

Mary quickly left for Elizabeth's house. When she arrived, she did not have to tell her cousin what had happened. Elizabeth, filled with the Holy Spirit, already knew. "You are blessed among women, and blessed is the child you will bear," Elizabeth said. "I am honored that the mother of my Lord should visit me!"

Mary said, "My spirit rejoices in God, my Savior. From now on, everyone will call me blessed, for God has done great things for me. He brings down the proud, and he lifts up the humble. He fills the hungry with good things, and he sends the rich away empty. In his mercy, he helps his people."

Mary stayed with Elizabeth for three months.

An Angel Speaks to Joseph

Matthew 1:18-25

When Mary returned from Elizabeth's house, she talked to Joseph. She told him about Gabriel's visit. She told him about Elizabeth's baby. And she told him that she also was going to have a baby.

Joseph did not know what to do. He did not want to marry her if she was having someone else's baby. But he did not want to shame her either. Maybe he could break up with her quietly.

One night an angel came to Joseph in a dream. "Don't be afraid to take Mary as your wife, " the angel said. "Her baby is from the Holy Spirit. She will give birth to a son, and you will name him Jesus. He will save his people from their sins."

When Joseph woke up, he obeyed the angel. He brought Mary to his home to be his wife. Together, Joseph and Mary waited for the promised baby.

No Room in the Inn

Luke 2:1-5

In those days, the emperor decided to count all the people he ruled. He ordered everyone to return to his or her hometown to be counted. Joseph and Mary had to travel to Bethlehem.

It took nearly a week to go from Nazareth to Bethlehem. When Joseph and Mary finally arrived, they saw people everywhere. Some were camping in the town square. Others had stopped by the side of the road.

"The inn is full," someone told them.

Mary was tired. She knew it was time for her baby to be born.

Joseph went up to the inn and knocked on the door. He told the innkeeper that Mary was going to have a baby.

"I'm sorry," said the innkeeper, "but we don't have any rooms. We don't even have any quiet corners where she could lie down."

"What will we do?" asked Mary.

"I don't know," said Joseph.

Jesus Is Born!

Luke 2:6-7

Behind the inn, there was a cave; and inside the cave, there was a stable where travelers kept their animals. The stable-cave was quiet, warm, and dark.

"Let's go into the stable," Joseph said. "We can make a bed on the straw. It's better than sleeping outside."

During the night, Mary's baby was born. Mary wrapped him in long strips of cloth to keep him warm. She made a bed for him in a manger full of straw.

Mary remembered Gabriel's words: "You will have a son, and … he will be King forever." She wondered what the angel meant.

Why would a king be born in a stable instead of a fine house?

Why would a king sleep on scratchy straw in a feeding trough instead of on satin cushions in a cradle?

Why would a king's birth be greeted only by donkeys and chickens and little stray cats?

Angels Sing to the Shepherds
Luke 2:8-15

That night in the fields outside Bethlehem, some sleepy shepherds were watching their flocks of sheep. Suddenly an angel appeared before them, and dazzling light shone all around. The shepherds were terrified.

"Don't be afraid, " said the angel. "I bring you good news of great joy for all people. Today in Bethlehem, your Savior has been born. This is how you will know him: you will find a baby wrapped in strips of cloth, lying in a manger."

All at once, the sky was full of angels singing praises to God:

"Glory to God in the highest, and peace on earth to those with whom he is pleased!"

Then, as quickly as they had come, the angels disappeared. Once again the sky was dark. But the shepherds were wide awake.

"Let's go to Bethlehem," they said to each other. "Let's see this baby that God has told us about."

15

The Shepherds Visit the Baby

Luke 2:16-20

Mary and Joseph were resting in the stable when they heard footsteps and loud talking. "This must be the place, " someone said. "At least it has a manger."

Several rough-looking men and boys came through the doorway. "There he is," one said, pointing at the newborn baby.

" 'A baby, wrapped in strips of cloth, lying in a manger.' That's what the angel told us," said another.

"This is the Savior," said a young shepherd boy. "This is the Lord."

The men and boys knelt down before the baby.

Then the shepherds nodded to Mary and Joseph and ran out of the stable. Mary could hear them shouting, "Glory to God in the highest!" She could hear them telling everyone they met that the Savior was born.

The Savior, Mary thought. *The Lord. The King. The Son of God. ... Who is this child of mine?*

Mary and Joseph Bring Jesus to the Temple

Luke 2:21-38

Mary and Joseph named the baby Jesus, just as the angel had told them to do. They took Baby Jesus to the temple to present him to the Lord.

Near the temple lived an old man named Simeon. The Holy Spirit had told Simeon he would not die until he saw the Savior. One day, the Holy Spirit told Simeon to go to the temple. When he arrived, he saw Mary and Joseph and Jesus.

Simeon took Baby Jesus in his arms. He said, "Lord, now I can die in peace, for I have seen your Savior, a light for the whole world."

At the temple lived a very old woman named Anna. Anna was a prophet. When she saw Baby Jesus, she gave thanks to God. Then she began to tell people that the Savior was born.

Mary and Joseph were amazed at what people were saying about Jesus.

The Wise Men Follow a Star

Matthew 2:1-6

In a distant, eastern land lived some wise men. They studied holy books, and they knew that a mighty King would soon be born. They studied the sky, and one night they saw a new star.

"The King is born," they said. "Let us go worship him."

The wise men gathered together much food and water and many rich gifts. They followed the star for many months. They passed through wide, empty deserts. They climbed high mountains. They crossed deep rivers.

When they got to Jerusalem, the wise men stopped. They asked everyone, "Where is the newborn King?"

In Jerusalem, the priests and scholars had also been studying the Scriptures. "The Bible says that Israel's ruler will come from Bethlehem," they said.

Bethlehem was only a few miles from Jerusalem. The wise men got ready to see the new King.

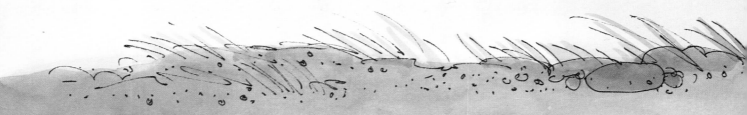

The Wise Men Visit Jesus
Matthew 2:9-11

That evening the wise men looked at the sky. Once again they saw the star. It was shining over Bethlehem.

They left immediately for the little town. Now the star shone directly over a house. Could this be where the new King lived? It did not look like a palace.

The wise men went up to the door and knocked. Inside they found the baby Jesus with Mary, his mother. The wise men bowed down and worshiped the little King. Then they gave him the gifts they had brought.

They gave him gold, because he was a King who would rule the world.

They gave him incense, because he was a Priest who would bring people to God.

And they gave him myrrh, because he would die to save people from sin.

When the wise men left the house, they were full of joy. They had seen the Savior of the world.

The Farmer and His Seed

Matthew 13:1–23; Mark 4:1–20; Luke 8:4–15

A man went out to plant a field. As he walked along, he scattered seeds on the ground.

Some seeds fell on the hard ground beside the path. Birds quickly snatched them away.

Some seeds fell on rocky ground. They sprang up quickly, but they didn't grow deep roots. When the sun shone hot, the young plants withered and died.

Some seeds fell on thorny ground. They started to grow, but the thorns grew even faster and choked the plants.

Some seeds fell on good soil. They grew deep roots and strong, green leaves. When the plants were big and healthy, they produced much fruit.

The Lost Sheep
Matthew 18:12-13; Luke 15:1-7

A man had a hundred sheep. Some were big and some were little. Some were black and some were white. Some were fast and some were slow. He loved each one of them.

26

Every day the man took his sheep to a pasture where they could eat fresh green grass. Every day he took them to a stream where they could drink clear cold water. Every night he counted them to be sure they were all safe.

One night he counted only ninety-nine sheep. The night was cold and stormy. The man was tired and hungry. But one of his sheep was missing.

The man turned around and went back to the pasture and the stream. He looked up cliffs and down canyons. He looked everywhere until he found the lost sheep.

The man called his friends and neighbors. "Let's celebrate," he said. "I have found my lost sheep."

The Runaway Son

Luke 15:11–32

A man had two sons. The older son was obedient.
The younger son was not.
    The younger son took lots of money and left home.

He spent the money foolishly. Soon it all ran out.

The boy got a job feeding pigs. He was so hungry he wanted to eat the pigs' food. "I could get a better job at my father's house," he thought.

The boy returned home. His father ran out to meet him. "I'm a bad son—," the boy began, but his father interrupted.

"Let's have a party!" he said. "My son has come home!"

The older son was angry. "Why don't you give me a party?" he asked. "I have always obeyed you."

"Everything I own will be yours someday," his father replied. "But today, let's celebrate. I thought my son was dead, and he is alive!"

The Two Builders

Matthew 7:24-29; Luke 6:47-49

A wise man decided to build a house. "I will build on solid rock," he said. "It will never move or crumble."

"The man ordered bricks. He hired workmen. After

many months, his house was finished.

A foolish man also decided to build a house. "I will build on a sandy beach," he said. "It is easy to build on sand."

The man ordered lumber. He hired workmen. In just a few weeks, his house was finished.

The storms came. It rained and rained. The wind howled. The sea swelled up, and giant waves battered the beach.

High above the sea, the rock did not move. The wise man's house stayed snug and safe.

Down on the beach, the sand began to slip and slide. The foolish man's house trembled and tottered. Then, with a crack and a crash, it slid into the sea.

The Wedding Feast

Matthew 22:1-10; Luke 14:16-24

A king planned a great feast for his son's wedding. He invited all the great people of the land: princes and merchants, generals and landowners.

The wedding day came. The king sent his servant to call the guests. But when the servant returned, he was alone. The guests had refused to come.

"I must inspect my new land," said one.

"I must try out my new oxen," said another.

"I must spend time with my new bride," said a third.

The king was angry. He told his servant, "Go back

into town and invite the poor, the crippled, the blind, and the lame."

The servant did as the king commanded. He returned with many guests.

"There is room for still more," said the king. "Go out on the open road and invite migrants and tramps and the homeless. My house will be full for my son's wedding feast."

33

The Rich Man and Lazarus
Luke 16:19-31

There was once a rich man who wore silk and ate pheasant every day.

At his gate lay a poor man named Lazarus. Lazarus was sick, but nobody nursed him. He was hungry, but nobody fed him. The rich man paid no attention to him at all.

Lazarus died, and the angels carried him to Abraham's bosom. The rich man also died, but he was taken to a place of torment.

The rich man looked up and saw Abraham and Lazarus. "Father Abraham!" he cried out. "Send Lazarus to dip his finger in water and cool my tongue."

"I cannot send him," said Abraham. "No one can cross from one side to the other."

"Then," said the rich man, "send him to warn my five brothers, so they do not come here too."

"They have Bibles," Abraham replied. "If they don't read the Bible, they won't listen to Lazarus either."

The Pharisee
and the Tax Collector

Luke 18:9-24

Two men went to the temple to pray. One man was a Pharisee; the other, a tax collector.

The Pharisee was a religious leader. He was known for being good. People respected him.

This is how he prayed:

"God, I thank you that I am not like most people. I am not greedy, unfair, or unfaithful. I pay tithes on all I

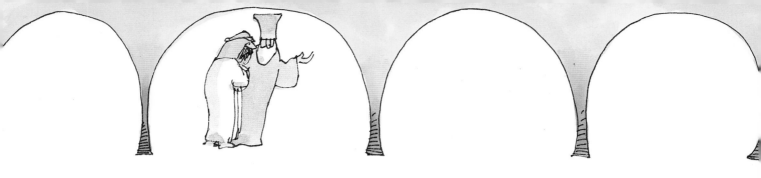

get. I fast twice a week. I am nothing like this tax collector."

The tax collector was a traitor. He was known for cheating. People hated him. He was ashamed of himself, and he stood as far away from the Pharisee as he could.

This is how he prayed: "God, have mercy on me, for I am a sinner."

God forgave the tax collector. He did not forgive the Pharisee.

The Good Samaritan

Luke 10:30-35

A man was traveling from Jerusalem to Jericho when some robbers jumped out and attacked him. They took everything he had. Then they beat him up and left him beside the road to die.

A priest came down the road. He saw the dying man. He crossed to the other side of the road and looked the other way.

A Levite came down the road. He saw the dying man. He crossed to the other side of the road and walked quickly by.

Then a Samaritan came down the road. He saw the dying man and felt sorry for him. He cleaned and bandaged his wounds. He helped him onto his donkey. He took him to an inn and paid for a room.

"Take good care of him," the Samaritan said to the innkeeper. "If you need more money, I will give it to you on my way back."

The Workers in the Vineyard

Matthew 20:1-16

Early one morning a man went to the marketplace to find workers for his vineyard. "I will give you one denarius a day," he promised.

At nine o'clock the man returned to the

40

marketplace and hired more workers. "I will give you a fair wage," he said.

At noon, at three o'clock, and again at five o'clock the man hired still more workers.

When evening came the workers were paid. Those who began work at five o'clock got one denarius each. So did those who began work at three o'clock, at noon, and at nine o'clock.

The workers who had come at daybreak expected more money. They had worked longer than anyone else. But each of them got one denarius.

"This is unfair," they grumbled.

The man said, "Didn't we agree on one denarius? Is it unfair to you if I am generous to the others?"

The Rich Fool

Luke 12:16–20

Once there was a man who had a very good harvest. He had so much grain that he did not know what to do with it.

He sold some and bought everything he had ever wanted.

He sold some more and piled up bags of money in every room of his house.

And he still had mountains of grain left.

"What shall I do?" he said to himself. "I don't have room for all this."

He thought and he thought. "I know," he finally said. "I will tear down my little barns and build bigger ones. I will put my things and my money and my grain in my new big barns. And then I will retire. I will eat and drink and have a good time."

But God said, "You fool! Tonight you will die, and then who will enjoy your riches?"

Jesus Says No to Satan

Matthew 4:1-11; Mark 1:12-13; Luke 4:1-13

Jesus had spent forty days in the wilderness. He had not eaten any food, and he was hungry.

One day Satan came to him. "If you are God's Son," said Satan, "turn stones into bread."

Jesus answered, "Scripture says that God's Word is more important than bread."

Satan then took Jesus to a high place. "If you are God's Son," he said, "jump off, and let God save you."

Jesus answered, "Scripture says, 'Don't put God to a foolish test.'"

Then Satan showed Jesus all the kingdoms of the world. "These kingdoms are mine," he said. "Worship me, and I will give them to you."

Jesus answered, "Get out of here, Satan! Scripture says, 'Worship only God.'"

Jesus knew he was God's Son. He knew that the whole world belongs to God. He would not do any miracles for Satan. He would do them only for God.

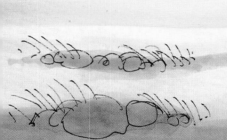

Jesus Turns Water into Wine

John 2:1-12

There was a wedding at Cana in Galilee. Mary, the mother of Jesus, was invited, and so were Jesus and his disciples.

In the middle of the feast, the wine ran out. Mary said to Jesus, "They have no wine." Then she said to the servants, "Do whatever Jesus tells you."

Nearby were six huge stone jars. Jesus said to the servants, "Fill the jars with water."

The servants filled them to the brim.

"Now dip some out," said Jesus, "and take it to the man in charge of the feast."

When the man tasted what the servants brought him, he was amazed. He went to the bridegroom and said, "Most people serve the good wine first, but you have kept the best wine for last!"

This was Jesus' first miracle. When his disciples saw it, they believed in him.

Jesus Calms the Storm

Matthew 8:23-27; Mark 4:35-41; Luke 8:22-25

It was evening, and Jesus was tired. "Let's cross the Sea of Galilee and rest," he said to his disciples.

The men set sail. Jesus lay down in the back of the boat and fell asleep.

Suddenly a fierce wind arose. Huge waves crashed against the little boat. Water poured over the sides, and the boat began to sink.

Jesus was still fast asleep. The disciples called out to him, "Don't you care that we are drowning?"

Jesus got up. He faced the howling wind and roaring waves. He raised his arm and said, "Peace! Be still!"

Instantly the wind stopped. The waves flattened out. The night was calm and still.

Jesus turned to his disciples and said, "Why were you afraid? Where was your faith?"

The disciples were amazed. They said to each other, "Who is this man? Even the wind and the sea obey him!"

Jesus Casts Out Demons

Matthew 8:28-34; Mark 5:1-20; Luke 8:26-39

There was a wild man living in a graveyard near the Sea of Galilee. Night and day he ran naked across the mountains, screaming. People said he had a demon.

One day the man saw Jesus. He ran to him and knelt down. Jesus knew that many demons lived in the man. He ordered them all to leave.

Nearby was a herd of two thousand pigs. "Send us into those pigs," the demons said.

Jesus agreed. Suddenly the pigs began to scream. Then they stampeded down the mountainside into the sea.

Many people went out to see what had happened. They found the wild man sitting next to Jesus. The man was wearing clothes. He was talking quietly.

Frightened, the people begged Jesus to leave. The wild man asked Jesus, "May I go with you?"

"No," said Jesus. "Stay here and tell everyone what God has done for you."

Jesus Heals a Paralyzed Boy
Matthew 9:1-8; Mark 2:1-12; Luke 5:17-26

In Capernaum lived a boy who could not walk.
His friends put him on a stretcher and took him to
Jesus.

People packed the house where Jesus was
preaching. They blocked the door and the windows.
The men could not get inside. So they climbed onto
the roof, removed some tiles, and lowered their friend
through the opening.

Jesus saw that the boy had faith. "Son," he said, "your sins are forgiven."

Some people whispered to each other, "Only God can forgive sins!"

"Which is easier to say," Jesus asked them, "'Your sins are forgiven,' or 'Get up and walk'? I will show you that I can forgive sins."

Jesus turned to the boy. "Get up, take your stretcher, and go home," he said. The boy got up and ran through the crowd.

The people were amazed. They said to each other, "We have never seen anything like this!"

Jesus Raises Jairus's Daughter
Matthew 9:18-19, 23-26; Mark 5:21-24, 35-43; Luke 8:40-42, 49-56

One day a ruler named Jairus came to Jesus and knelt down. He said, "My only child is dying. If you will lay your hand on her, she will live."

Jesus started to follow Jairus, but soon a messenger ran up. "Sir, your daughter has died," he said. "There's no need for Jesus to come now."

Jesus kept on walking. "Do not fear; only believe," he said.

When they arrived at Jairus's home, they could hear people crying. "Why weep?" Jesus asked. "The girl is not dead. She is sleeping." The people laughed at him.

Jesus went with the girl's parents into her room. He reached out and took her hand. "Little girl, get up," he said.

Immediately the girl sat up and got out of bed!

"Give her something to eat," Jesus said.

Soon everyone for miles around was talking about the raising of Jairus's daughter.

Jesus Feeds Five Thousand
Matthew 14:13-21; Mark 6:30-44; Luke 9:10-17; John 6:1-14

Wherever Jesus went, huge crowds followed. They wanted to hear him teach. They wanted to see him heal. Sometimes they forgot all about eating.

Late one afternoon, the disciples said to Jesus, "It's time to send the people away to buy food."

Jesus replied, "Why don't you give them something to eat?"

The disciples did not have any food. Andrew said, "There is a boy here with five barley loaves and two fish, but what are they among so many?"

"Bring them here to me," Jesus said.

Jesus took the boy's food. He gave thanks for it, broke it, and gave it to the disciples.

The disciples started passing out the bread and fish. The more they gave away, the more they had! There was more than enough bread and fish for the whole crowd.

The people said to one another, "Jesus really is the prophet we have been expecting."

Jesus Walks on Water
Matthew 14:22-33; Mark 6:45-52; John 6:15-21

The disciples finished gathering up the leftovers from the meal of loaves and fishes. Jesus told them to take their boat and cross the Sea of Galilee. He stayed behind to say good-bye to the crowd. When he was finally all alone, he went to a quiet place to pray.

That night the wind was strong and the waves were high. The disciples rowed for many hours. They were tired.

Suddenly they saw a man walking on top of the sea. He was coming straight toward them. "It is a ghost!" they cried out.

Then they heard a familiar voice. "Don't be afraid," Jesus said. "It is I."

Jesus climbed into the boat with the disciples. Immediately the wind died down, and the boat arrived safely at its destination.

The disciples were amazed. "Truly you are the Son of God!" they said.

Jesus Heals Ten Lepers

Luke 17:11-19

In Jesus' day, people with leprosy could not live with their families. Wherever they went, they had to shout, "Unclean! Unclean!" so people could stay away from them. Most lepers never got well.

One day ten lepers met Jesus. "Jesus, Master, have mercy on us," they called out.

Jesus said to the ten lepers, "Go and show the priest that you have been healed."

The lepers looked at their bodies. Marks of leprosy were still there. But they believed Jesus, and they set off to find the priest. While they walked, their leprosy disappeared!

One of the lepers immediately turned around and ran back to Jesus. He knelt at Jesus' feet. "Thank you, Jesus," he said.

Jesus helped the grateful man stand up. "I healed ten men," he said. "Where are the other nine? Are you the only one who is praising God for being healed?"

Jesus Promises More Miracles

John 14:1-14

Jesus and his disciples were eating their last meal together. Jesus would soon be going home to his Father in heaven. The disciples were worried. They did not know what would happen to them.

Jesus saw that his friends were lonely and confused. "Don't be afraid," he said. "My Father has been doing wonderful things through me. When I leave, he will do even greater miracles through you. He will do whatever you ask in my name."

Soon the disciples understood Jesus' words.

In Jesus' name, they healed the sick, raised the dead, and cast out demons.

In Jesus' name, they told the whole world that the Father loves us, that Jesus died for us, and that the Spirit gives us life.

From their day to ours, millions of people have followed Jesus. And that is the greatest miracle of all.

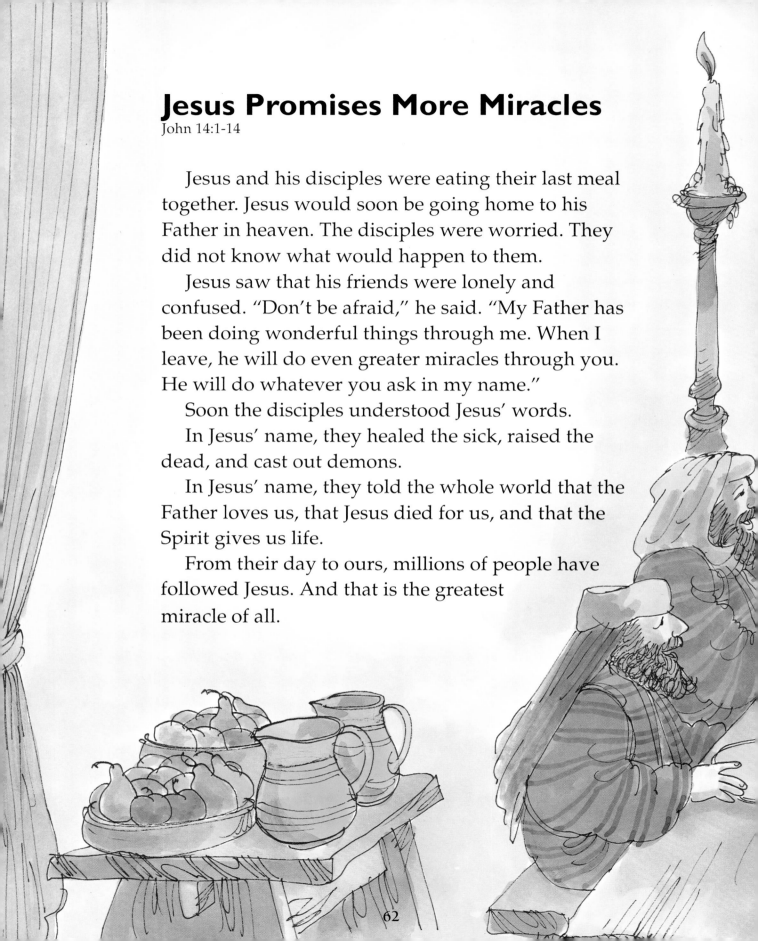

A Parade for Jesus
Matthew 21:1–11; Mark 11:1–11; Luke 19:28-38; John 12:12-19

It was Passover time, the biggest feast of the year. All God's people were going to Jerusalem to celebrate.

"Go find a colt that has never been ridden," Jesus told two of his friends. "Untie it and bring it to me."

Jesus' friends brought him the colt and helped him climb on. Jesus and the colt started down the road to Jerusalem.

People on their way to the feast saw Jesus and the colt. They remembered that he had healed their friends. They remembered that he had taught them about God. "Hosanna!" they cried out.

They threw their coats into the road to make a path for Jesus.

Children ran beside Jesus and the colt. "Hosanna!" they sang.

They threw palm branches into the road to make the path green and beautiful.

"Jesus is king!" the people shouted. "Blessings on the one who comes in the name of the Lord!"

The Last Supper

Matthew 26:17-35; Mark 14:12-31; Luke 22:7-23

Peter and John prepared the Passover supper for Jesus and ten of their friends. The thirteen men met in an upstairs room.

Jesus took some bread. He said a blessing, broke the bread, and gave it to his friends. "Eat this," he said. "This is my body. Do this in memory of me."

Then Jesus took a cup of wine. He gave thanks and passed it to his friends. "Drink this," he said. "This is my blood. It will be poured out to forgive sins."

His friends whispered to one another, "What is he talking about?"

"Some people do not want me to be king," Jesus said. "One of you will betray me to my enemies."

"Not me," said Peter.

Jesus looked sadly at Peter. "Before the rooster crows," he said, "you will say three times that you do not know me."

The Garden of Gethsemane
Matthew 26:36–46; Mark 14:32-42; Luke 22:39-46

Judas left supper early. He went to tell Jesus' enemies where to find Jesus.

Jesus and his other friends sang a hymn. Then they went to a garden called Gethsemane.

Suddenly Jesus felt sad and afraid. "Stay here," he said to his friends. He walked farther into the garden and threw himself onto the ground. "My Father!" he cried out. "Do not make me suffer and die! But I will do your will, not mine."

After a while Jesus went back to his friends. They

were fast asleep. "Could you not stay awake and pray for an hour?" Jesus asked. Then he left them and kept on praying.

A second time Jesus returned to his friends. Again they were asleep. "Why are you not praying?" Jesus asked.

The third time Jesus did not ask his friends to pray. "Get up!" he said. "My enemies have come to to arrest me."

Soldiers in the Garden
Matthew 26:47-56; Mark 14:43-52; Luke 22:47-53; John 18:1–11

Jesus' friends woke up suddenly. They saw flaming torches. They heard shouts. They saw Jesus and Judas walking toward each other.

Judas kissed Jesus. A crowd of angry men rushed at Jesus, waving swords and clubs. "Judas," Jesus said quietly, "are you betraying me with a kiss?"

Peter ran to Jesus' side. He drew his sword and struck out at the men. One man fell back, grabbing the right side of his head.

Peter's sword had cut his ear off.

"Put your sword away, Peter," Jesus said. "If I needed help, I could ask my Father, and he would send me hundreds of angels."

Then Jesus reached out and healed the man's ear.
The men took hold of Jesus and led him away.
Jesus' friends were terrified. Would they be captured
too? All eleven of them turned and ran for their lives.
Jesus was alone with his enemies.

Peter's Sin

Matthew 26:57-75; Mark 14:53–72; Luke 22:54–71, John 18:25–27

Peter followed Jesus from a safe distance. He saw him go into the high priest's palace. Peter went into the courtyard.

He heard the high priest say, "Tell us if you are the Son of God."

He heard Jesus answer, "I am who you say I am."

He heard the leaders say, "Jesus deserves to die."

A servant girl asked Peter, "Aren't you one of his followers?"

"I don't know what you're talking about," said Peter.

Someone else said, "You were with Jesus."

"I don't even know the man," said Peter.

Another person said, "You talk just like Jesus."

Peter cursed. "I do not know him!" he shouted.

Just then a rooster crowed. Peter remembered Jesus' words: "Before the rooster crows, you will say three times that you do not know me."

Peter burst into tears and ran outside.

The Trial

Matthew 27:1-32; Mark 15:1-22; Luke 23:1-32; John 18:28—19:16

The crowd shouted, "Crucify him!"

The governor, Pilate, was puzzled. "He has done nothing wrong," he said.

The crowd roared louder, "Crucify him!"

"Do you want me to crucify your king?" asked Pilate.

"Caesar is our only king," the people cried.

Pilate washed his hands. "I am innocent of this man's blood," he said. "Do whatever you like."

The soldiers beat Jesus. They spat on him and pushed a crown of thorns onto his head. They knelt before him, chanting, "Hail, King Jesus!" Then they put a heavy wooden cross on Jesus' bleeding back.

Jesus took a step and stumbled. He took another step and fell.

A soldier saw an African man, Simon of Cyrene, in the crowd. "Come and help," he ordered, placing the cross on Simon's shoulders.

The crowd moved toward Golgotha, the place of the skull.

The Crucifixion

Matthew 27:33-56; Mark 15:23-41: Luke 23:33-49; John 19:17-30

The soldiers pounded big nails through Jesus' hands. They dropped the cross into a hole in the ground.

The crowd made fun of Jesus. "He said he was God's chosen one," they said. "Let's see him save himself!"

Two thieves hung on crosses next to Jesus. One

thief said to him, "Remember me when you come into your kingdom."

"I promise you," Jesus said, "that today you will be with me in paradise."

Mary, Jesus' mother, stood near the cross with Jesus' friend John. Jesus said to Mary, "John is now your son." He said to John, "Mary is now your mother."

The sky turned black. For three hours there was no light. "God," Jesus cried out, "why have you deserted me?"

Suddenly the earth began to rumble and shake. "It is finished," Jesus said. "Father, into your hands I commit my spirit."

And he bowed his head and died.

He Is Risen!
Matthew 27:57–28:8; Mark 15:42–16:8; Luke 23:50–24:8

Friday afternoon a rich man, Joseph of Arimathaea, took Jesus' body, wrapped it in a clean cloth, and put it in his own new tomb. He rolled a heavy stone across the doorway.

Saturday morning Jesus' enemies said to Pilate, "We are afraid Jesus' friends will steal his body."

Pilate sent soldiers to guard the tomb. Jesus'

enemies sealed the tomb so nobody could move the stone.

Early Sunday morning some women went to the tomb. They planned to put spices and perfumes on Jesus' body.

Pilate's soldiers were not guarding the tomb. The heavy stone was not blocking the doorway. The women tiptoed inside.

The tomb was empty!

Suddenly the women saw a man in shining clothes. "Why are you looking in a tomb for a living person?" the man asked. "Jesus is not here. He is risen! Go quickly and tell his friends the good news!"

Seeing and Believing

Luke 24:9-12, 36-49; John 20:19-21

The women ran to tell Jesus' friends. "Jesus is alive!" the women said.

The men did not believe them. Peter and John ran to the tomb to see for themselves. It was just as the women had said. The tomb was empty.

What could this mean? Had Jesus' body been stolen? Would they be blamed? Jesus' friends were frightened. They hid in a room and locked the door.

Suddenly Jesus was in the room. "Peace be with you," he said.

The door was still locked. Were they seeing a ghost? "Touch me," said Jesus. "A ghost does not have flesh and bones."

The men timidly reached out and touched Jesus. He was warm. He felt real.

"Is there anything here to eat?" asked Jesus. The men gave him a piece of grilled fish. Jesus ate it hungrily.

The men looked at each other and smiled. "He is risen!" they shouted.

Jesus Forgives Peter
John 21:1-19

Peter, John, and five other men had fished all night. They had caught nothing.

At daybreak they saw a man standing on the shore. He called out, "Throw the net on the right side of the boat." They did, and fish swarmed in.

"It's Jesus!" John said. The men turned toward shore, where Jesus was cooking fish over a charcoal fire.

After breakfast Jesus turned to Peter. "Peter, do you love me?" he asked.

"Yes, you know I love you," said Peter.

"Peter, do you love me?" Jesus asked again.

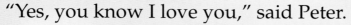

"Yes, you know I love you," said Peter.

"Peter, do you love me?" Jesus asked a third time.

"You know everything," said Peter. "You know I love you."

Jesus smiled, and suddenly Peter understood. Three times Peter had said he did not know Jesus. Now Jesus was forgiving him.

"Follow me," said Jesus. And Peter did.